MY FIRST
INDOOR GARDEN

Everything You Need to Know
to Grow Little Houseplants

FOR PHANTHIRA, MY PRETTY PRINCESS FROM THAILAND...
THANK YOU TO CHARLÈNE, VÉRONIQUE, AND JULIETTE!

First English translation copyright © 2021 by Skyhorse Publishing, Inc.

Terrariums, cactus, carnivores.... Je fais pousser mes petites plantes
© First published in French by Rustica, Paris, France – 2013

Sky Pony Press books may be purchased in bulk at special discounts for sales promotion, corporate gifts, fund-raising, or educational purposes. Special editions can also be created to specifications. For details, contact the Special Sales Department, Sky Pony Press, 307 West 36th Street, 11th Floor, New York, NY 10018 or info@skyhorsepublishing.com.

Sky Pony® is a registered trademark of Skyhorse Publishing, Inc.®, a Delaware corporation.
Visit our website at www.skyponypress.com.

10 9 8 7 6 5 4 3 2 1

Manufactured in China, July 2021
This product conforms to CPSIA 2008

Library of Congress Cataloging-in-Publication Data is available on file.

Cover design provided by Éditions Rustica
Cover illustration by Charlène Tong

Print ISBN: 978-1-5107-6393-7
Ebook ISBN: 978-1-5107-6394-4

Philippe Asseray
Illustrations by Charlène Tong
Translated by Grace McQuillan

MY FIRST
INDOOR GARDEN

Everything You Need to Know
to Grow Little Houseplants

SKY PONY PRESS

Sky Pony Press
New York

CONTENTS

TOOLS I NEED

Gardening indoors doesn't mean you don't need tools! They just won't be the same ones you would use in the vegetable patch. . . .

A tray to keep dirt from getting everywhere

When you are handling plants and dirt at home, you might get a little dirty, even if you're very careful. It's easier not to get dirt everywhere if you use a plastic potting tray with raised edges.

Spoon and fork

To make potting soil mixtures, fill pots, or clean your plants' roots, you will need a small garden fork and spade. But even the smaller versions of these gardening tools might be too big for you, so it is probably best to use an old fork and spoon from the kitchen.

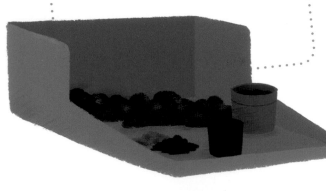

Make sure you ask your grown-ups before using the fork and spoon for gardening!

A small watering can

To water your plants, you will need a watering can. Choose one that is small, easy to fill at the kitchen sink, and easy to pick up without spilling.

A nice little shower!

A small spray bottle

To moisten the leaves of certain plants that might be too hot inside your house, or to gently water the soil after planting seeds, use a small spray bottle.

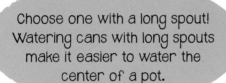

Choose one with a long spout! Watering cans with long spouts make it easier to water the center of a pot.

Gloves

Potting soil is black and can stain. Contact with certain plants may irritate the skin and cause a rash. You don't have to wear gloves, but you can if you want to.

A variety of pots

Gather pots in different sizes and shapes. It is very important to make sure that they all have at least one drainage hole in the bottom so any extra water can escape after you water.

ARRANGING MY INDOOR GARDEN

As you know, all plants grow outside—some grow in places where it is never cold, but they are still always outside. To keep them alive in your house, you will have to try to give them everything they would have if they were outside . . . .

Saucers under pots

Saucers are used to collect the water that the soil cannot absorb and that drains through the holes in the base of the pot. Saucers prevent flooding and keep your bedroom from getting dirty!

And clay pebbles in the saucers

Plant roots hate when the soil is soggy and full of water. This is why you should always use pots with at least one drainage hole in the bottom. This is also why you should fill the saucer with clay pebbles and place the pot on top of them. This way, even if the saucer is full, the soil will not turn into a sponge.

Now the pot won't make a nasty stain on the table.

My plants are leaning toward the window

What plants miss the most when they are inside is light. You might think there is enough light to play or walk around your living room, but for plants, it's almost completely dark! Remember that they should always be fewer than six feet away from a window—otherwise, they will bend over trying to get closer to where the light is coming from.

Littles in the back, big ones in the front!

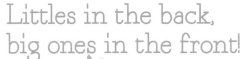

Always keep your plants together. To make sure you can observe and care for all of them, and so that they can all enjoy the light, use shelves of differing heights. This way, the little plants will not be in the shadow of the bigger ones.

My indoor garden on wheels

If you have several plants and want to make it easier to clean your living room or bedroom, you can place them all in a cart, small wheelbarrow, or wagon.

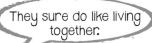

They sure do like living together.

TAMING A CARNIVOROUS PLANT

Carnivorous plants are not dangerous, and there's no risk of getting bitten! In fact, they are quite easy to grow, and the traps they set to capture insects are extraordinary!

THE MOST FASCINATING OF ALL : THE VENUS FLYTRAP

It catches insects. But how???

Its leaves resemble an open mouth. On the inside of the leaves are three hairs. When an insect slips between the leaves and touches two hairs at the same time, the "mouth" immediately closes. The insect is trapped.

Testing the flytrap

We are not always lucky enough to be nearby when a Venus flytrap catches an insect, but you can force the trap to close and see how quickly it reacts. Gently place a blade of grass inside the "mouth." As soon as two of the hairs have been touched, the leaf will close. But be careful: this is not a game and is not something you should be doing all the time.

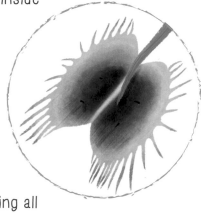

How does it eat the insect?

The plant does not swallow the insect; it instead produces substances that will dissolve it into a liquid. This liquid then passes into the plant through the Venus flytrap's skin.

To help your plant grow better, divide it in two

Set up a table covered with a plastic covering. Turn over the pot with your Venus flytrap inside, holding the plant between your fingers. Then pull off the pot. With your hands, gently separate the plant roots and replant them right away in other pots filled with blond peat moss that is already very moist.

Plants love humidity

The air inside a house is dryer than the air outside, and your carnivorous plants may have a hard time. If you don't have a terrarium, place your pot or pots in a saucer about 1 inch tall filled with expanded clay pebbles sitting in rainwater. The saucer should be three times as wide as the pot.

How should I water it?

The best water for carnivorous plants is rainwater. Ask your grown-ups if you can collect rainwater that comes out of the drainpipes on your house. Keep the water in the house for at least 24 hours so it can reach the temperature of the room your plant is in.

THE BUTTERWORT: A STRANGE CARNIVORE

This is a plant that doesn't look like other carnivorous plants because it doesn't appear to have any traps. It also blooms almost all year long and produces lots of flowers. This is probably what confuses the insects!

Odd leaves

Its leaves form a kind of rose pattern on the ground, which makes the plant look like lamb's lettuce (you know, the one that grows in the vegetable garden) with thick leaves.

How does it catch insects?

The butterwort looks like a typical garden plant that insects can land on without having to worry. But its leaves are lined with tiny glands that can't be seen with the naked eye, and they slowly release a greasy substance that sticks to unsuspecting insects' feet.

The "Weser" butterwort blooms from spring until autumn.

It's spitting out glue!

The right soil for my butterwort

This plant is not like other carnivorous plants. It does not grow in sphagnum moss, and instead prefers a mixture of equal parts of perlite, vermiculite, pozzolana, and sand.

To make this mixture yourself, look for the above materials at gardening centers or hardware stores.

Taking cuttings from my plant

In the winter, carefully tear off a few leaves from the ones growing on the outer edge of your plant. Their base should be almost white. Pour some of your butterwort soil mixture into a container and lay these leaves flat on top of the soil. Press down a little bit on the white part to encourage roots to appear.

The leaf will make roots and form a new plant.

OTHER FUNNY CARNIVORES

These two carnivorous plants are very sneaky and hide their traps in order to capture curious insects more easily. Take a moment to learn about them because they are not only interesting but also easy to grow indoors!

Drosera capensis

This little plant never grows taller than 8 inches, and the traps it uses are its long, thin leaves. On the tip of each leaf are hairs where little drops of glue collect. Insects are attracted to these drops, which they think are made of water, and they quickly find themselves stuck. The plant then produces its famous substance to dissolve the reckless bug.
This is a plant that grows quickly, and unlike certain plants that need to be moved out of your living room or bedroom to somewhere cooler in the winter, it never needs to change rooms.

Sarracenia minor

Its leaves form a vertical funnel 20 to 28 inches tall with a kind of cover called an urn or a pitcher. Under this hood are nectar glands that attract insects and make them very confused as soon as they drink the nectar. After consuming the nectar, the insects fall into the bottom of the funnel where water and bacteria digest the plant's meal. The inside of the tube is lined with hairs pointing toward the bottom to keep the insects from climbing back up.

This plant thought of everything!

In some *Drosera* species, the drops of "glue" are red, and in others they are transparent.

Creating a terrarium

If your grown-ups have an old aquarium they're no longer using, you can turn it into a miniature garden for carnivorous plants.

Along the bottom, spread a 2-inch layer of pozzolana (rocks made out of volcanic ash) and cover this with a piece of gardening felt. Next, add the soil for your plants. Use special soil for carnivorous plants or Chilean sphagnum moss dampened with rainwater.

You will need a layer that is 6 to 8 inches thick. Now you can plant your favorite plants.

Don't force them to eat!

Some captured insects look like they're not moving

When a carnivorous plant eats an insect, there is nothing left behind except for the insect's skin, which is too hard to be dissolved by the plant's digestive liquid. The plant has absorbed the inside of the insect and the rest will be carried away by the wind or will disintegrate by itself.

Does my plant have enough insects to eat?

Don't worry, carnivorous plants are plants, first and foremost, with roots that can draw food out of the ground. This means that they don't need a lot of insects. A mosquito or a fly from time to time is more than enough for them. Don't try to catch insects to feed them—you might cause your plants to die of indigestion!

A WATER LILY AT HOME!

Water lilies are plants that grow in the bottom of ponds and lakes. But some of them, like the Nymphaea hybrid species, are originally from tropical regions and must be grown at home as indoor plants ... they are often the prettiest water lilies, too!

How does a water lily grow?

A water lily's leaves and flowers look like they're floating on the surface of the water, and in fact they are, but they are also connected by stems to a central root. The water lily is a plant that grows in the soil underneath the water.

What kind of pot should I use for my water lily?

A water lily must be planted in water! Ask your grown-ups to buy a large bucket or plastic tub, at least 3½ gallons. A big black plastic bucket as wide as it is tall would be perfect for your water lily.

Use a very big bucket!

Preparing the bucket

Even though water lilies grow in water, their roots are still anchored in the ground, so create a mixture using dirt from your yard and potting soil for aquatic plants. Make sure you have equal amounts of dirt and potting soil. Pour your mixture into the bucket and fill it a quarter of the way. Then cover completely with pebbles.

Fill the bucket with rainwater

Tap water may contain things your water lily won't like, so it's better to use rainwater. This is easy if your grown-ups have a cistern or rain barrel near the drainpipes. Gently pour the water over the pebbles to fill the bucket without stirring up the dirt.

Choose wisely!

Make sure to buy a water lily that grows in shallow water!

Planting my water lily

First, roll up your sleeves! Stick your hands in the water and pull out a few pebbles from the middle of the bucket. Submerge your plant and push the roots into the dirt. Put the pebbles back in place. They will help the plant stand up while the roots anchor themselves to the soil.

Can I put it outside?

Yes, as soon as the temperature is no longer going to dip below 60°F, you can put your bucket outside in full sunlight. Just remember to add a little water every day to replace any that evaporates.

MY PREHISTORIC DESERT PLANT

This is the perfect plant to impress your friends. It may look dead, but it is able to open and return to its original green color in just a few hours.

So, what is this strange plant?

It is known as the rose of Jericho. But it's not a rose at all, at least not like the ones you're used to seeing or smelling in the yard, and it doesn't come from the city of Jericho in Palestine. It actually looks more like a head of lettuce with fern-like leaves, and it grows in a desert in northern Mexico! Like ferns, it does not produce any flowers and its "seeds" are spores that appear on its leaves.

Where does it live?

This plant lives in very dry soil and even on rocks, without any soil at all! In fact, its usual companions are members of the cactus family.

Prehistoric?

Experts have discovered ancestors of the rose of Jericho that are estimated to be 400 million years old. Back then, they grew as large as actual trees.

It can live without water for a very long time

Cactus plants form a trunk that they use for water storage, and it is easy to see why they are able to live many months without water.

What a weird-looking lettuce!

For the rose of Jericho, it's a little different: As soon as it rains and the ground is wet, it opens and forms a cup. Then it closes itself up, folding its leaves to keep the humidity inside. Then it can live in slow-motion, nice and easy, without wasting its precious water supply.

How to make it open in only a few hours ...

1 In the morning, after your friends have arrived, place your rose of Jericho in front of them in a shallow, empty bowl. Pour a little water into the bowl and go play.

2 Come back a few hours later. The strange brown ball that was all dry before has opened up and turned green!

Another "camel plant": the tillandsia (or air plant)

This plant grows outside of the ground on trees or rocks. It absorbs water through its leaves instead of through its roots— and it produces flowers! You can attach it to a piece of tree bark and hang it from a shelf or bunk bed.

MAKING A HYACINTH BLOOM FOR THE HOLIDAYS

The hyacinth is a fast-growing plant that can bloom inside your house one month after being planted in a pot. All you need to do is cool it down in November.

What is a hyacinth?

A hyacinth is a flower that comes from a bulb, like a tulip, narcissus, or a crocus. It is planted in the garden in October or November and it blooms in the spring. It is usually very fragrant.

How to make the hyacinth think that it's winter...

The hyacinth blooms in the spring, after its bulb has been exposed to a cold period. To make it bloom in your house in time for the holidays, put the bulb in the produce drawer of your refrigerator during the second half of November and leave it there for about two weeks.

When you take the bulb out of the refrigerator and it feels the warm temperature of your house, it will think it is spring and will start to bloom.

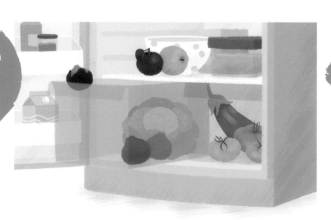

Cool down!

Plant the bulb in a pot

1 In the beginning of December, fill a clay pot with a mixture of equal parts garden soil and sand. Leave 1½ inches between the top of the soil and the top of the pot. Water just a little.

2 Take the bulb out of the refrigerator and place it in the middle of the damp soil, with the pointy tip facing up. Pack your soil-sand mixture around it until half of the bulb is covered. Place the pot in a saucer near a window.

Monitoring your hyacinth

Very quickly, you will see leaves and then a bundle of flowers appear out of the top of the bulb. Water around the bulb regularly to feed the soil and to make the pot heavier and more stable. To prevent the stem holding the flower from leaning too far toward the window, rotate the pot a quarter turn every day.

> The hyacinth will lean toward the window to benefit from the sunlight.

A sweet-smelling winter

To enjoy the smell of these flowers for a longer time, place a hyacinth bulb in the refrigerator every two weeks beginning in early November.

I CAN GROW AN AVOCADO!

The avocado plant grows naturally in Central America. Where we live, we eat the fruit of this plant after removing the pit.

Saving a pit

In the summer, if your grown-ups are planning on eating avocado, ask them to keep one or two of the pits. Rinse them under the tap to get rid of any green flesh that is still attached. Dry with a paper towel.

When the pits are completely dry, they are easier to hold and won't slip out of your hands.

Place your pit in water to sprout

Find an empty plastic bottle. Ask an adult to cut the base 3 inches from the bottom and to make a second cut 3 inches below the top. Ask them to remove the cap.

1 Now it's your turn: place the upper part, without the cap, upside down inside the bottom part. Press down a little so the two parts fit tightly together. Pour water into your setup until some of the liquid rises up into the part that looks like a funnel.

2 All you have to do now is place an avocado pit in the bottom of the funnel with the pointy part facing up. Be careful: the water should only touch the bottom of the pit. Check the water level every day and add more if needed.

The first roots appear after a few weeks...

Be careful! The young roots are very fragile!

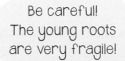

Moving your new plant to a pot

1 When the roots are 1½ to 2 inches long, you can take your pit out of the funnel and plant it in a pot filled with soil. Handle your pit carefully so you don't break the fragile roots.

2 Ask your grown-ups for a clay pot 5 to 6 inches wide and fill it two-thirds of the way with potting soil for indoor plants. Hold your pit in one hand so the roots are touching the soil, then slowly add more soil until half of the pit is buried. Water just a little to help the soil stick to the roots.

3 Before long, the pit will split in half and a stem will grow out of this crack. You are watching your avocado tree being born! Place the pot near a window.

Cut off its head several times!

When the plant reaches 8 to 12 inches in height, ask for a pair of shears to cut the stem ½ inch above a leaf. Two new stems will appear. You will trim these later on, and then you'll have four new stems.

If you don't trim your avocado tree, it will still grow but it will only have one stem and will not be very pretty.

Other plant pits you can sprout

The avocado is not the only plant you can try growing from a seed. This also works with pumpkin seeds or even the seed inside a mango pit. The only difference is that you can plant them directly in the soil.

I'M GROWING PEANUTS!

You've had peanuts as a snack before, of course! But what you may not know is that they come from the peanut plant, a plant that you can grow at home to harvest your own peanuts! Doesn't that sound fun?

Sprouting seeds in cotton

Ask your grown-ups for two cotton pads. In the spring, place three peanut seeds between the two pads and pour a little warm water on top to soak the cotton. One week later, gently remove the top cotton pad. The seeds should have started to sprout.

Planting the seeds in a bowl

1 Find a pot, old baking dish, bowl, or any other container around 15 inches wide that will hold around 3 inches of soil. Make a hole in the middle of the soil as big as the palm of your hand and 1 inch deep.

2 Place your sprouted seeds flat on top of the soil, leaving plenty of space between them. Cover them with soil and use your hand to pack it down a little bit, being careful not to damage the sprouts. Water carefully to make sure the soil is damp.·

The seedlings look a little like clover plants.

Monitoring my young plants

Place your pot in a warm part of the house, somewhere where the temperature is at least 68°F. The best spot is on top of a radiator. Check every day to make sure the soil is moist. It should not be waterlogged, but always damp. If you need to, add a little water.

Be patient! It will take 3 or 4 weeks for the seedlings to appear. When they have all stuck their noses out, place the container near a window. Peanut plants need a lot of light.

The flowers bury themselves!

Your plants will grow to about 12 inches tall. Then they will produce pretty yellow flowers. If the weather is warm, you can take the container outside.

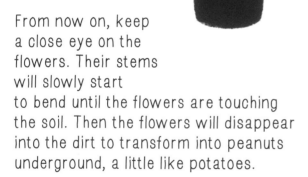

From now on, keep a close eye on the flowers. Their stems will slowly start to bend until the flowers are touching the soil. Then the flowers will disappear into the dirt to transform into peanuts underground, a little like potatoes.

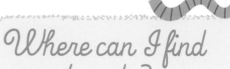

Where can I find peanut seeds?

The roasted peanuts you find at the supermarket will not sprout! You have to buy peanut seeds at a pet shop. These seeds are part of the diet of birds like parrots. You don't need to buy a whole pound of them, though—a few peanut seeds is enough!

What a show!

The flowering stems are leaning down and connected to the soil, a little like the cables that hold up a circus tent.

Harvesting your peanuts

When the leaves are totally wilted, usually in October, you can harvest your peanuts. Just hold the plant and gently pull it out of the soil. You should find a few peanuts mixed in with the roots. They look like the peanuts you buy in their shells, but yours are a whitish color because they have been grown away from the light and are not roasted.

Serving your peanuts

To eat your peanuts, you must roast them first. Ask an adult to heat the oven to 350°F. Line a baking sheet with parchment paper, shell your peanuts, and spread them out on the tray. Place the tray on the middle oven rack and cook for 25 minutes.

Take the peanuts out of the oven and transfer them to a container. Sprinkle a little salt over them while they are still warm and wait for them to cool down before serving!

ROCKS THAT BLOOM!

No, these aren't real stones, but they are plants that look like little rocks. Like cactus plants, they grow naturally in places where rain is scarce. You can enjoy growing them at home in a pot or bowl.

Living stones?

These plants are called "living stones" because they are often gray and mottled like the stones found around them in nature.

These plants do not have stems and are often made up of a single pair of leaves low to the ground. This helps the plant expose less of itself to the sun's rays and allows it to stay cool!

They bloom every year and produce one or several pairs of new leaves.

Succulents?

The leaves are called "succulents" because they are thick and full of water.

Planting living stones

1 Place your living stone in a shallow clay pot. It should be shaped like a cup and must have at least one hole in the bottom to allow water to escape. Choose a pot just a little bigger than your plant.

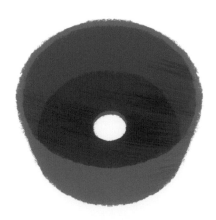

2 Take your plant out of the plastic container you probably bought it in, and use a fork to carefully scrape off the dirt around the roots.

4 Next, water your plant a little bit so the soil sticks to the roots. Not too much! Half a glass of water is enough.

3 Now, pour potting soil into your new pot and place your plant inside, spreading the roots out in every direction. You will need special soil made for cactus plants.

Dry soil

For living stone plants, it's best if the soil dries quickly in the pot.

Splitting up your stones to share with friends

1 After two or three years, your plant will have formed other pairs of leaves. Remove it from the pot and scrape off the soil around the roots with an old fork.

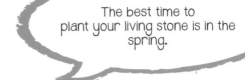

The best time to plant your living stone is in the spring.

2 Carefully separate the pairs of leaves. To do this, take one pair of leaves in each hand and gently pull them apart without damaging the roots. It's okay if a few roots break.

Since your living stone plant produces new leaves every year, eventually it will have quite a lot of them! Share!

3 Now immediately replant each new plant in its own pot, just like you did at the beginning with your first plant. Don't forget to use soil for cactus plants and also to water them a little bit! You can give these living stones to your friends or trade with other people who are also growing strange plants.

A few living stone plants that are easy to grow

Conophytum wettsteinii is an interesting plant with pale green leaves and crimson flowers that appear on top of them.

Conophytum x marnierianum is very easy to grow. Its leaves have brown spots and it has yellow and crimson flowers.

Pleiospilos nelii has leaves with small, dark green spots and large, pale yellow flowers.

Lithops aucampiae has mottled brown leaves and golden yellow flowers.

Conophytum wettsteinii

Lithops aucampiae

MY SHY PLANT FOLDS ITS LEAVES WHEN I TOUCH IT

Mimosa pudica is a plant that behaves in an odd way. When something brushes against one or more of its leaflets, the small leaves instantly fold inward. It is the most common sensitive plant, but other sensitive species display a similar reaction.

Why does it react this way?

This is actually a defensive reaction against animals that may want to eat it! By folding its leaves, it becomes much less appetizing. This completely normal phenomenon happens naturally. The warmer it is, around 75°F, the faster the leaves will fold. The leaf returns to its original shape after a few minutes, but the unfolding happens so slowly that it is difficult to observe.

Planting your sensitive little seeds

In the spring, prepare some potting soil using peat moss, sand, and compost and use it to fill a pot. Place a few seeds on the surface and water gently with rainwater. Place the pot near a radiator, and make sure the soil is always a little damp. Over the course of the summer, your plant will develop pink pom-pom flowers.

Is the bathroom the best place for my shy plant?

Sensitive plants appreciate warm areas with plenty of humidity in the air, so the bathroom is a good place as long as it has a window.

If this is not an option, you can also plant them in the terrarium where you planted your carnivorous plants.

TRIVIA

What mammal can sometimes be found trapped by a carnivorous plant?

1. A field mouse
2. A squirrel
3. A cat

Answer: 1. Small rodents like field mice sometimes fall into the urns of large pitcher plants.

MUSHROOMS ARE SOMETIMES FOUND GROWING IN A CIRCLE. WHAT IS THIS PHENOMENON CALLED?

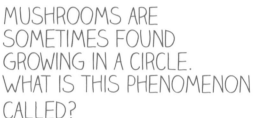

1. A mushroom round
2. A witches' circle
3. A fairy ring
4. Saturn's ring

Answer: 2 and 3. Mushrooms are the visible part of the plant, a little like a flower, attached to an underground white thread called the mycelium. If a mushroom spore (a "seed") falls in a favorable location, it develops a mycelium that spreads in all directions. A mushroom will form at the end of each thread, eventually creating a circle.

Can a bulb grow if it is planted upside down or on its side?

Answer: Most bulbs have one end that is positive than the other that should be facing up when it is planted. This point is where the new stem will appear. However, the bulb can still grow if it is on its side. The stem will still come out and will straighten up to emerge out of the soil.

How wide are the leaves of the largest water lily in the world?

1 0.30 yard

2 1 yard

3 3 yards

Answer : 3. This giant water lily lives in the warm waters of the Amazon in Brazil.

What is the name of the other bulb plant that, like the hyacinth, blooms in the springtime, sometimes even through the snow, and has white bells?

1. Lily of the valley

2. Star-of-Bethlehem

3. Snowdrop

Answer : 3. The snowdrop, as you may have guessed from its name! It is a small plant that grows in clumps with drooping, bell-shaped white flowers.

THE BOTANICAL NAME FOR THE SENSITIVE PLANT WE LEARNED ABOUT IS MIMOSA PUDICA, BUT THE BOTANICAL NAME FOR THE MIMOSA TREE (THE ONE WITH YELLOW FLOWERS THAT SMELLS GOOD IN THE WINTER) IS NOT MIMOSA. WHAT IS IT?

1. Acacia

2. Grevillea

3. Nandina

Answer : 1.

The avocado seed you planted comes from a tropical plant. In addition to a pot inside your house, where else can it grow?

1 Inside large greenhouses in botanical gardens

2 In outer space

3 On the island of Corsica

Answer : 1 and 3.

CREATING A MINIATURE CACTUS FOREST

Cacti are easy plants to grow at home—even in your bedroom. They often have funny shapes and can be part of a collection you can share with other people. They may be prickly, but only if you get too close!

How to pick up your cactus without getting pricked

Take a sheet of newspaper and fold it into a thick strip. Wrap it around your cactus, hold it in place, and use one hand to squeeze the ends of your band together. Now you can remove it from the pot.

Moving your new cactus to a different pot

Cactus plants are almost always sold in small plastic pots. You will have to change the pot if you want the cactus to live for a long time. Gently pull it out of its plastic pot.

Using a small fork, carefully scrape off any dirt that is stuck to the roots. Place your cactus on the table.

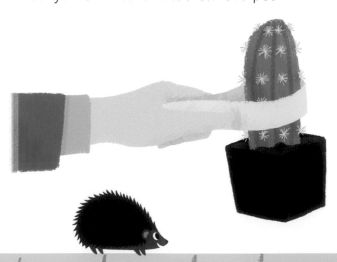

Planting your little cactus in its pot

The right soil

Cactus plants will not grow in pure potting soil or in dirt from your yard. In your pot, you should put a special soil just for cactus plants that your grown-ups can find at a garden center. You can also make some yourself by mixing two handfuls of sand, one handful of dirt from the yard, and one handful of the potting soil your grown-ups use for their houseplants.

1 Choose a ceramic pot. Fill it one-third of the way with gravel. This will help the water escape quickly through the hole in the bottom.

Wait before watering!

Make the mixture yourself!

2 Hold your cactus over the pot with its roots in the air. Lean it to one side so you don't get pricked while you finish filling the pot with soil.

Creating a cactus forest

If you like cacti, you might enjoy planting several of them together in a flat container like an old baking dish. Just ask an adult to make a hole in the bottom first. Fill the container with gravel and your homemade mixture. Then plant your cactus plants, but not too close together. You can even place a few large stones on top of the soil to make it look like a real desert landscape.

3 Now straighten it up and press down with your fingers all around the base. Do not water it! Wait about a week before giving it a little water.

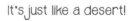

It's just like a desert!

A cactus with flowers that glow

Here's a round little cactus that should amaze your friends! Not only does it produce funny little yellow flowers, but these flowers glow in the dark! Its name is Notocactus graessneri . . . But it is not easy to find. Your grown-up will have to find it on the Internet.

Taking care of your cactus plants

First learn how to water them: only once a month, no more, submerge the pot for fifteen minutes in a large bowl. That's it! In addition, you should dust your cactus plants using a new paintbrush with long bristles. This can also be done once a month.

GROWING MUSHROOMS IN MY HOUSE

To grow mushrooms at home, first you will have to ask your grown-ups to buy a box filled with a special soil containing developed button mushroom spores and dirt. Mushrooms don't come in packets of seeds like radishes do.

Preparing the soil in your box

Open your box. In it you will find another box. This is where you are going to dump the soil, which we will call "compost." The mushroom spores are in this compost. After you have transferred the compost to this box, leave it open and place it in a room where the temperature is between 68° and 77°F.

Monitoring your baby mushrooms' growth

After three days, cover the compost with the dirt provided in the box and place the lid on top, leaving it half-open.

When you see the mycelium (roots) appear, the best thing to do is place the box in the basement.

Over the course of a week or more, thin white "roots" called mycelium will grow out of the compost and enter the dirt layer. From these roots, the mushrooms will start to grow. When the mycelium is visible on the surface, place your box in a cooler part of the house where the temperature is around 60°F.

The baby mushrooms are here!

Make sure the dirt doesn't dry out. You can moisten it every day using a small spray bottle. After about a week, the first mushrooms will appear. They are fragile when they are this small, so don't touch them yet! Keep spraying the box every day and watch your mushrooms grow.

Harvesting your mushrooms!

You can harvest your first mushrooms a week after they come out of the ground. Here's what you need to do: carefully hold the mushroom cap between two fingers and gently turn it to remove it from the mycelium. Now you can carefully take it out of the ground.

Where can I find these mushrooms?

An adult can order mushrooms from websites such as: www.northspore.com or www.mushroomadventures.com

Let the mushrooms grow before touching them.

MY PLANT'S SEEDPODS EXPLODE TO RELEASE ITS SEEDS

This plant is ticklish and very sensitive! If you touch its seedpods with your finger, they will burst open and release their seeds. Be careful! It's not dangerous, but it is truly spectacular to watch.

What is this strange plant?

From July to October, the Himalayan balsam has pink and white flowers that turn into seedpods after they wilt. These seedpods are set up a little bit like catapults. When the seedpod is fully grown, it opens suddenly and flings the seeds up to two yards away from the plant. This is why this plant is considered an invasive species and why we often find large quantities of it in the same place.

Planting Himalayan balsam seeds

Prepare a mixture of equal parts potting soil and dirt from the yard. Use it to fill a pot that is at least 6 inches deep. Place two or three seeds on the surface and push them down just a little bit without covering them. Water carefully. Using a small spray bottle is best.

The Himalayan balsam is an annual plant. The seeds that fall from its pods will sprout in the spring.

Caring for your exploding plant

Place your pot outside in the shade and make sure the soil always stays damp. To make sure you don't forget to water it, leave the spray bottle next to the pot and get in the habit of watering your seedlings every morning before you go to school.

To make the fun last longer, you can plant seeds every month from April to June.

Enjoy exploding the seedpods between your fingers . . .

The seedpods are long and end in a tiny point. To make the Himalayan balsam react and force it to release its seeds, gently pinch the seedpod between your thumb and index finger on the side opposite the little point. The seeds will be projected forward.

The first flowers will appear two months after the seedlings.

You can keep the Himalayan balsam seeds for other plantings.

A DANCING PLANT

This is a funny plant that moves whenever there is noise or light. To delight your friends, make it wiggle to the sound of your voice or with a flashlight!

What is this bizarre plant?

This plant is originally from southern Asia and botanists call it Desmodium motorium or Desmodium gyrans. Some of its leaves move almost constantly in order to capture as much sunlight as possible, and they go so fast that you can see them doing it!

Sprouting seeds

Place four or five seeds on a cotton pad. Place the pad flat on a small saucer, then pour a little water onto it to moisten it. Leave the saucer near a radiator because these black bean-shaped seeds need heat to sprout. Be patient—sometimes the seedlings wait three weeks to come out!

Where can I find this plant?

You can order this dancing plant from websites such as: www.worldseedsupply.com or www.rarexoticseeds.com.

Make sure you always keep the cotton pad a little damp.

Planting your dancing plant in a pot

This plant grows best in acidic compost. Ask your grown-ups if they have a bag with a little bit left inside. Use it to fill a pot and poke three holes in the compost to form a triangle, making sure the holes are not close together. The holes should be as deep as your fingernail. Place one sprouted seed in each hole. Cover with compost, then water with a spray bottle filled with rainwater.

Acidic compost?

Azaleas and rhododendrons love this kind of soil, too.

How to make its leaves move

Bring a flashlight close to your plant and move it all around. The leaves will immediately start turning to try and follow the light.

You can also make them move by playing music close to the plant.

Your plant needs light

When the plant starts to grow, place the pot near a window or on the porch. It will need lots of water in the summer, but make sure the water doesn't stay in the compost and make it soggy! Don't forget to place the pot in a large saucer filled with clay pebbles or gravel.

Don't leave the plant sitting in water!

TRIVIA

YOU MAY HAVE CREATED A CAC-
TUS GARDEN IN YOUR BEDROOM,
BUT DO YOU KNOW THE DIA-
METER OF THE WIDEST CACTUS
TRUNK IN THE WORLD?

1. 0.30 yard

2. I yard

3. 1.50 yards

*Answer: 3. The largest cactus plant is found in
Mexico. It is called the cardon cactus. It can mea-
sure more than 15 yards tall, and its main trunk can
grow to over 1.50 yards wide! The body of the plant
forms an enormous barrel that can hold 10 tons of water, enough to resist the dry weather for several years.*

I sometimes grow in the
desert, I am green, and
covered in spines . . . but I
am not a cactus. What am I?

*Answer: I am a spurge, a plant that looks like a cactus.
My sap is always toxic, so you should avoid touching me.*

What peanut-based dish is very
popular in Thailand?

1. Egg rolls

2. Pad Thai

3. Spring Rolls

*Answer: 2. Thai stir-fried noodles, known as
Pad Thai, are famous all over the world!*

The Himalayan balsam is not the only plant that releases its seeds in a unique way. Do you know what the squirting cucumber does?

1. It makes stinky farts to keep birds from eating its seeds.

2. Its seedpods fall to the ground and explode like farts.

3. It makes a noise when it releases its seeds.

Answer: 2. This strange cucumber is inedible and pro-duces small seedpods that fall off as soon as you touch them. Then they burst open to release their seeds.

IS TAKING MY INDOOR PLANTS OUT IN THE YARD GOOD FOR THEM?

Answer: Yes, of course. But don't take them outside if the temperature is higher than it is inside your house or if there is a heat wave. Also, when you do take them outside, always place your plants in the shade and away from the wind.

What is the connection between cactus parasites and . . . yogurt?

Answer: Cactus plants are sometimes attacked by small, floury-looking insects called "cochineals." They are not dangerous for your cactus if there are only a few of them. These insects contain a red substance that is used to add red coloring to foods we eat every day . . . like yogurt, for example!

PLANTS EAT LIGHT

Did you know that plants can't live without light? In fact, they are unable to "digest" in the dark. They don't have stomachs like us or like other animals, but their leaves are food factories that only function with light.

How do plants feed themselves?

Roots draw in the basic ingredients that a plant needs from the soil, water, or air. But this food is usually not ready to eat right away, and it has to be transformed. Each plant basically has their own built-in kitchens for this purpose.

Leaves: plant kitchens

Amazing, isn't it?

In its leaves, the plant cooks the liquid that the roots have drawn in. There aren't any ovens in these leaf kitchens, though. Instead, light automatically transforms the liquid from the roots into food that will be sent to every part of the plant, including the roots.

Indoor plants can't see the sun

This is why you should always place indoor plants near a window so they can enjoy as much light as possible and feed themselves.

Even if you give them fertilizer, they won't be able to use it if they aren't getting enough light.

Can ceiling lights help?

No. First of all, the lightbulbs in the ceiling are too far away from the plants, and they also give off a somewhat yellow light that plants cannot use to make food.
In a pinch, you can place a lamp near your plants but use a special "daylight" bulb.

What part of the house gets the most light?

Rooms with big windows or sliding glass doors will give your plants the most light. But remember that once a plant is 6 feet away from the window, and even if you don't notice it, it is already missing out on half of the sunlight it would get outside.

WATERING MY INDOOR PLANTS

As you know, dirt and soil dry out very quickly in pots. You will have to water your plants more often than you would if they were planted in your yard. But be careful: roots also don't like it when there is too much water.

Potted plants like taking baths

To be sure that the soil is damp even in the middle of the pot, put your pot in a small tub and fill it with water until water is covering half of the pot. The water will slowly enter the hole in the bottom of the pot and soak the root ball all the way through. This process is called "capillary action."

A watering can

The watering can is the most practical tool for watering each pot. Choose one that is small. It won't hold a lot of water, but it is lighter than a large one and much easier to handle.

A spray bottle

If you don't have a small spray bottle, ask your grown-ups to save a spray bottle of window cleaner once it is empty. Rinse it well several times and fill it with water. The spray bottle lets you gently dampen the leaves of your potted plants. This removes dust and helps cool them off in the heat. You can also use this spray bottle to water seeds you have planted without having to worry about damaging the soil.

Pour slowly!

A little shower?

A long spout

Choose a watering can with a long spout. Not only will it be easier to reach the root ball at the base of your plants, but it will also help you water slowly. This will give the dirt or soil enough time to absorb the water.

A very practical accessory

If you want to be sure your potted plants are getting enough water, you can use a different tool found in garden centers. It's a porous ceramic cone, and all you have to do is screw a bottle of water onto it. Push the attached cone and bottle vertically into the soil and water will slowly seep out through the cone to give the plant plenty to drink.

The best time to water

Indoor potted plants don't rest during the cold months and need to be watered all year long. Just reduce the amount of water by half—even though they aren't resting, they are still living at a slower pace. The best time of day to water your plants is always the morning. And don't forget to let the soil dry a little before watering it again.

FEEDING MY LITTLE PLANTS

Plants eat while they drink! This is because they find the nutrients they need in water. In the dirt in your yard, plant roots manage to find food all by themselves. In a pot, however, there isn't enough soil and you will have to give them some fertilizer.

How can I tell if a plant is hungry?

A plant always "says" it's hungry with its leaves: you will see some of them fold up and then become soft and droopy. They might turn pale or yellow, then they will fall off. It's best not to wait until your plant is hungry before you feed it.

How often should I feed it?

This depends on the plants, their size, and the kind of fertilizer you are giving them. Look at the instructions on the label when you buy your plant and follow the directions on your package of fertilizer. You should never use too much fertilizer because it can kill the plant.

Don't give your plant too much fertilizer—it may get indigestion.

MAKING YOUR OWN FERTILIZER

Crush some seashells

If you eat oysters or mussels at home, save the empty shells after the meal. Rinse them with tap water to get rid of any leftover meat and, more importantly, the salt from seawater. Once dry, place them in a tub on the patio and crush them with a small hammer that an adult has given you permission to use. Now you can spread these tiny pieces of shell over the dirt in a flowerbed. They will decompose and leave behind plenty of good things for the plants.

Super banana peels!

The banana is a delicious fruit that you probably already love! Among other things, its skin contains nutrients that help the plant produce flowers and fruit. After eating a banana, cut the peel into small squares on your plate. You can spread them around rose bushes or tomato plants. Use one peel for each plant.

You can make your own fertilizer out of food scraps!

Plants love eggs!

Let's just say that chickens put lots of wonderful things in their eggshells—things that are very useful for garden plants! On a day when omelettes are on the menu at your house, keep the shells and gently crush them into tiny pieces with a rolling pin on a cutting board. Sprinkle them over the soil in your pots and flower boxes whether they are in the yard, on the balcony, or in the house!

Grass tea

Grass contains a lot of nitrogen, which is a plant's favorite food. If you have a yard, the day the lawn is mowed, ask if you can keep half of the contents of the lawn mower bag. Empty this into a large tub and fill it with water until the grass is covered. A week later, remove the grass from the tub and throw it on the compost pile. Your herbal tea is ready! You can use it to water your plants by diluting 1 quart of your tea in about 2.5 gallons of water.

Diluting liquid fertilizer in your plant's water

Many fertilizers for potted plants are liquids that you have to mix with water before feeding them to your plants.

Check what is written on the bottle to know how much fertilizer you should mix with the water in a bottle or watering can. It's not always easy to do the calculations, so don't hesitate to ask someone older for help.

Fertilizer spikes to stick in the soil

In garden centers, you can also find fertilizer spikes that look a little like tiny candy bars.

If you don't have the supplies to make your own fertilizer, you can buy some in a specialty store.

Just push them into the dirt with your finger. When water from your watering can touches the spike, it will slowly dissolve, and the fertilizer will spread into the soil where the roots can reach it.

Read the instructions on the package carefully to know how many rods you should put in your pots, depending on how wide they are.

Fertilizer Spikes

Little balls to mix with the soil

You can also find fertilizer that comes in little balls. These work well and are very easy to use. They are usually brown or yellow and are sold under the name Osmocote.

During planting or repotting, just mix them into the soil, following the instructions on the box. When you water, the water will spread the fertilizer throughout the pot and transport it to the roots.

Fertilizer spikes are convenient, but sometimes the fertilizer only spreads around the spike and not throughout the entire pot.

REPOTTING MY PLANTS

After several weeks or months, dirt and soil start to wear out. Eventually they are no longer able to hold water, which contains the plant's food. You will have to replace the soil so your plants can continue to grow. This is called repotting.

Removing the plant from its pot

Stop watering your plant a few days before you repot it. This will make it easier to remove the pot. Place one hand flat on top of the pot, holding the plant between your fingers. Gently turn the plant and remove the pot with your other hand. If the root ball will not come out, tap the pot on the corner of a table.

Removing the old soil

Don't break the root ball—you don't want to damage the roots. You can, however, carefully scrape around the roots with a fork. This will make a little of the old soil fall off and unstick the roots a bit, which will help them spread out in the new soil.

Cleaning the pot

Brush the old pot well to get rid of the old soil. If it's a ceramic pot, you can place it in a tub filled with water. Ask an adult to add a little bleach to the water. This bath will help destroy any germs that might be hiding in the pot. Once dry, you can reuse the pot. You can throw away the old soil.

How often do I need to repot my plants?

You should change your plants' pots every three years. The best time for repotting your indoor plants is in early springtime. The longer days will stimulate their growth and they will be ready to form new roots.

Should I change the pot?

Changing the pot is a good idea. Your plants make new roots every day, and they will need more space as the years go by. Choose a pot that is a little bit bigger than the old one. This will give the plant plenty of room.

INDEX

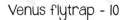